office peace

"*Barbara mixes new ingredients with zesty spices to concoct a recipe of delicious reading in the world of management and human relations. My margins were covered with scribbles and pages dog eared as I marked principles and concepts I want to think about and employ to make my work environment not only fun for me but for all those I have an opportunity to work with.*"

Jeff Wells – *Former CEO of Innovative Services of America and current CEO/CEM of Patagonia Holdings, LLC of Phoenix, Arizona*

"*The insights offered in* Office Peace *create a masterful work that rewrites the Golden Rule for transforming your company to a fun, healthy, and profitable organization. It is The Holy Grail of business transformation using the collective talents of your people in a fun, creative and safe environment.*"

Joe Weiner – *Vice President of Government Solutions, Knowledge Workers, and Top Banana Institute Disciple*

"*The concepts that* Office Peace *teach are valuable not only in business, but in every interaction we have with other human beings. I find the phrases 'diminish no one' and make 'no judgments' about other people's choices staying with me throughout the day. Plus, these thoughts bring a wonderful sense of peace and freedom.*"

Emily Hall – *Real Estate Broker/Small Business Owner*

office peace

your guide to a more respectful
(and more productive!) work environment

playfully by
Barbara Brannen
a fable

Denver, Colorado

office peace

your guide to a more respectful
(and more productive!) work environment

playfully by

Barbara Brannen

a fable

Published by:
Playmore
11988 West Cooper Drive
Littleton, Colorado 80127

Library of Congress catalog card number 2005904549

Published in the United States of America
ISBN 0-9761930-0-0

This book is dedicated to
Jim Cunniff *and* Jeff Wells.

Two people who have always known the heart and soul of work is in the way people are respected in their work. They showed me every day I worked with them the true meaning of work and the *joy* it could bring.

" *He has the power to render us happy or unhappy; to make our service light or burdensome; a pleasure or a toil. Say that his power lies in words and looks; in things so slight and insignificant that it is impossible to add and count 'em up; what then?*

The happiness he gives, is quite as great as if it cost a fortune. "

Charles Dickens – *Christmas Carol – 1907*

Contents

Acknowledgements

It is hard to know where to start to thank the wonderful group of people that follow here. I am so blessed to have the help and support of so many people, so if your name isn't here, and you were there for me, know that it is only old age and a short memory that kept you off this list.

First, my family; Michael, your unflagging support and sacrifices to make this book come to fruition are staggering. Christian and Patrick, your words when I was stuck or overwhelmed always calmed me and made the next thing happen. Mom and Dad for being there, letting me use the porch on hot summer afternoons and just loving me all the time.

Gail Kincade and Mo Hofmann, what can I say? You are simply the best. How is it that you never, ever give up on me?

Emily Hall, Cheri Knopinski, Jodie Brown, Lynne Zucker, Jane Kimball, Kathy Gangl, Bev Obenchain and my entire Fort Collins Abraham group, thank you from the top, bottom and middle of my heart for your love and support in this process.

Hae Won Kwon, you have once again done a yeoman's job of finding the right words when I didn't make sense. Allita Katzenbach, thank you so much for your work. Joe Biene, you took my calls and rose to the occasion when I was stuck.

Dick Bruso and Bill Frank, you held my hand and my heart when I needed it, and I will forever be in your debt for your encouragement and your kindness.

To Liz Williams, Dick Harrington, Jeff Dorsey, Jim Rohrer, Phil Kalin and Don Wingerter, you were amazing people to work with and I enjoyed every minute of it. You helped lead me to this book.

Jennifer Collins of Juniper Moon Studio did the marvelous cover art on this book. Jennifer, thank you so much for your artwork. Your wonderful sense of fun and joy gives beauty to this effort.

I am particularly blessed to have my book designed by the team of Debra Johnson and Lisa Scheideler at **shine, inc**. They took my words and made a beautiful book. You are fabulous to work with and I thank you for all that you have done to bring this book into reality.

1

Diminish No One

Once upon a time Sam started a new job in a new city at a new company called Top Banana Institute.

He had worked for four companies in fifteen years and always enjoyed his work. The only thing he ever struggled with was office politics. Usually he stayed away from difficult interactions, but sometimes things could really heat up during meetings. This was not a pleasant time for Sam.

A few weeks before, he had been interviewed and hired by a company in another city. While he never visited the eventual work location, Sam had high hopes for his new employer. The grapevine had it that this new office and company had conquered all office politics and actually worked under something called "Office Peace" as a motto.

While he didn't have the details he was skeptical that anyone could make an office free of politics. People cooperating freely seemed like a dream. Well, there was only one way to find out, he thought as he drove along. Go in and see what happens.

As Sam pulled into the parking lot he became unnerved as he could not find a place to park. There were two types of markings on the parking spaces. A few were marked "Distinguished Guest" and all the rest were marked "Employee of the Year." Since he was neither he drove around in confusion. Eventually, with more than a little guilt, he pulled into a parking space marked "Employee of the Year." He figured after checking in and finding out where all the other employees parked, he could move his car. Meanwhile there were plenty of spaces left for the obviously large group of people who won this award.

As he entered the lobby all his senses were engaged. He smelled apple pie and heard a piano being played. There was a waterfall going with a small pond and fish swimming around, even money at the bottom of the pool. Plants and brightly colored flowers were everywhere. Along one wall there was a bubble gum dispenser with the long curved slide that you see in toy stores, and next to that was a candy machine. Neither, he noted, required coins to dispense. Sam guessed those went really fast each day. Large colorful kites hung from the ceiling along with wall hangings that extolled the wonderful people who worked for the company and the great clients with which the company was privileged to work. Finally there was a beautiful statement about the honor the company felt to serve the world with their product.

"Sam," he heard in a loud pleasant voice, as a large woman of indeterminate age rushed towards him with her hand out. "We are thrilled you are here today. I hope your trip to our city was pleasant." Sam grasped the firm, warm hand extended to him and noted the large name badge that read Dottie.

"I did have a nice trip, thank you. I took my new boss's advice and saw some of the country along the way. He gave me some wonderful spots to visit with the time I had before I started."

"Great!" replied Dottie, "I hope your new home is suitable?"

"Yes," replied Sam, "I was surprised to find the refrigerator stocked and the basket of supplies and city information. I was starving when I got in and too tired to go out. It was a great relief."

Dottie then asked Sam the strangest question he had ever heard during a first meeting. "Would you mind if I gave you a welcome hug?"

Sam, while not a real hugging kind of guy said, "Sure, why not" and was immediately wrapped up in a big bear hug. Dottie quickly explained that the company was honored and grateful when people chose to join their team. They wanted to show it in every way possible. "If you had said no," Dottie noted, " I would respect that, too. However based on the type of people we look for and hire they almost always say yes because they know how to accept love and respect as well as give them." "As you can see, my name is Dottie and I want you to know that I will always be there for you when you ask for help, if it is humanly possible for me to do so."

Sam's head was spinning at this point. He wasn't sure if he had shown up for work or therapy. Overall he was feeling pretty good for some reason and ready to see more.

Dottie looped her arm through Sam's and led him across the lobby, where Sam noted a few employees playing a jazz version of chopsticks on the piano and laughing themselves silly.

"Before I forget," said Sam "I need to move my car."

Dottie smiled, asked where he had parked, and assured him it was fine just where it was. She smiled mysteriously when Sam indicated he didn't want to take an award winner's spot, and again Dottie told him he was fine parked where he was.

After a quick and painless processing of his ID and necessary payroll papers, Dottie handed him a badge like hers with his name in very large letters but with a large gold star in the corner. Sam inquired about the star and was told that it indicated that he was in his first week with the company. Sam noted that she also had a star but with a different color and asked if she was new as well. Dottie said no, she had been there for quite a while. Sam decided this was one of the strangest places he had been in and wondered what was in store next.

Dottie made a quick phone call to a colleague to cover the front desk for her. In a flash Mark showed up and introduced himself to Sam with a smile and a handshake.

"You probably already got the Dottie hug, so I'll spare you any further embarrassment," he chuckled. He fished in his pocket for a card and handed it to Sam with the comment that Sam should call his extension at any time with questions. He also added it would be his privilege to take him to lunch today. They arranged to meet at the front desk at noon and then Mark went to answer the front desk phone while Dottie steered Sam through the doors off the lobby.

As Sam entered the main area of offices he was taken by surprise. The entire place was well lit, with natural light pouring in through the offices on the exterior to the glassed-in offices in the interior. You could see from one end of the building to the other, yet the noise level was almost negligible. Bright plants and flowers again adorned every corner and creative, colorful balloons hung from the ceiling. It was almost like working outdoors, but somehow the glare of the sunlight was muted by the tinted glass on the side of the building. Eventually the ringing of phones, laughter and conversation made it into Sam's senses, but again he could not say it was overwhelming.

Dottie was watching him with a bemused expression, "Like what you see?"

"Well I'm not sure," said Sam. "It is definitely light and airy and fun, but there isn't much privacy is there?" "Well," said Dottie, "We are a company, which to us means we are a collection of people working together to do something great in the world. In order to accomplish that we have to work together. If we are all locked away behind walls, we may get work done, but it might not all fit together as it needs to. Let me give you a quick tour to show you how we create privacy for those who need it, and we know that some do."

Sam noted as they walked the corridors that each office was clearly marked with the first and last names of the people who worked in them, followed by a long large print statement of what that person did to make the company successful. Sam saw statements like, "I am the payroll clerk. My job is to see that each employee receives the correct pay for their work, that all appropriate governmental deductions are applied and that all benefits and other deductions are done accurately. My work is done to the best of my ability so that employees at the Top Banana Institute will not ever be distracted by an inaccurate check or any problems with their benefits or other deductions. Since mistakes can occur, my email is listed below and I will respond to your problem on the same day or my email will let you know when it may be longer."

Sam smiled and thought, "That is quite a commitment: Same day response? How does she do that?" Dottie smiled as she saw what Sam was thinking and explained that his orientation would answer many of the questions popping up in his mind.

Sam continued following Dottie through the company while she noted the location of the restrooms, employee cafeteria and several exits out of the building other than the main entrance. Dottie introduced Sam to Philip and Carol and indicated that they would be his orienteers for the day. She also indicated that each day throughout the week he would meet new orienteers. With a smile and a wave she headed toward her desk in the lobby.

Philip and Carol shook his hand and began walking along a corridor in the back, away from the offices. Sam could hear loud laughter coming from behind a closed door and music from another. Then there were several open doors. Carol motioned Sam into one of the rooms and to a seat at the table. Sam was overwhelmed by the room. Besides being bright and airy like the rest of the building, he was surrounded with toys, hats, beach balls and hula hoops. He noticed a smiley face outside this door, as well as on the closed doors he had passed.

Carol began, "Sam, we want to welcome you on behalf of all the employees and customers at the Top Banana Institute. We are honored that you chose us to be your employer and to share your gifts and talents with us. In the next few days we will orient you to our company and show you the underlying principles that make us not only a good company, but a great company. We want you to know that your work here is important to everyone. All functions in this organization are treated with respect whether you are the CEO or the janitor. No one person is more or less important than any other. Respect for one another is something you hear all the time, but in our organization we take it one step further. At no time and in no way will we ever diminish anyone. This applies to employees, vendors, our customers and anyone else that comes to our organization. Today your orientation will be about learning what this concept means and how you function with this intention. The reason we do this on the first day of orientation is to avoid even one negative comment about people and what they are or are not doing. Once someone says something that diminishes another, it can spread like a terrible virus and will never be repaired."

Philip jumped in at this point. "You have probably heard people say again and again that you need to forgive and forget, but we hope to take this a step further by never creating situations between people that require forgiveness or forgetting. Does this make sense to you?"

Sam blinked for a minute and then stammered, "I'm not sure I get what you are talking about but I like the idea that no one ever has to be diminished. I've seen too many good employees hurt by office gossip."

Philip smiled and continued, "I'm glad you agree that this is a good thing. It is not only about office gossip, though. It is about when people offer ideas, make mistakes and may not be working up to par. We have created a climate in this organization in which you do not dwell on what people have done wrong. We focus on what can be done to fix the problem and where lessons can be learned and applied. Even when someone offers an idea that you are sure will never work, you honor that idea. One of the ways we do this is by avoiding, when possible, using the word 'but.'"

"'But?'" Sam inquired. "'But,'" said Phillip with a grin. "'But' is a word that basically negates what a person has said. Instead we chose to use 'and' or 'or.' In this way we honor what the person has said and then add new ideas to theirs. The idea is to grow thoughts rather than negate and replace thoughts. Thoughts that grow organically, one to the other, are always more powerful and have more energy because everyone has a little piece of what they offered in them."

"I guess I never looked at 'but' that way, and it makes sense." Sam offered.

"Think how often you have felt diminished when people have responded to your ideas negatively," Carol added.

Sam paused for a few moments and thought about it. He knew that he was able to take criticism well. He also knew that there was an uncomfortable feeling right after the comment, and he tended to be a little quieter after the person spoke up, particularly in meetings. "I would love to know that I was never holding back, however I have noticed that sometimes after someone has 'but'-ted me I do tend to shut down a little," Sam confessed.

"Exactly," cried Carol. "And we don't ever want that to happen here. Everything everyone says has value, even if it doesn't exactly fit at the moment. Who knows, a week from now it may be the brilliant answer to a different situation. We work hard to see that no one is ever diminished by what we say. People here feel free to offer unusual and different ideas to situations, and we get a lot of good things going very quickly and easily. We also go home at night able to say, 'I diminished no one today.' This is probably the best feeling in the world. We worked hard, played together well in the sandbox and honored each other in our words and in our actions."

Sam's head was swirling. Wasn't orientation about who, how, where, why and what we do? Why was this concept the focus of an entire day of orientation?

Philip could feel Sam's uneasiness and confusion, remembering his own first day at the Top Banana Institute. It wasn't natural not to criticize.

It was supposed to be healthy to create challenge in the organization so things will be well thought out. Only after many months of watching this concept in action had Philip been fully convinced. He knew there were only so many words that he could use to describe this idea. He then came up with an idea of his own. "Let's drop in on the meeting next door so you can watch this concept at work. I happen to know they are working on the new marketing campaign for the latest version of the Top Banana's *Don't Get Mashed* video, and there are many diverse opinions about which is the best way to go," Philip offered.

Sam, Carol and Philip headed into the meeting room next door. "Sorry to interrupt, but we are demonstrating 'diminish no one' to a new employee. We were wondering if we could observe your meeting to help illustrate the concept," asked Philip. "Of course," responded the man standing at the front of the room wearing moose ears. Stretching his hand out to Sam he introduced himself and all of the other people in the room along with a description of their role in the meeting.

The meeting reconvened with lively discussion about whether comedy, safety, drama, simplicity or high definition computer graphics would be best for the first marketing of this new product. Sam watched in awe while all ideas were given nods and placed on the white board walls of the room. The group was making remarkable progress very quickly, and colorful markers distinguished different concepts. At one sticking point someone reached for a beach ball, tossed it to someone who had been more silent and asked for her thoughts. Rather than being offended or put off, the woman blurted out a very silly comment. The group quickly white boarded it and asked for more information. She said she had been silent while thinking along another line not yet brought up. A discussion of this new line followed for about five minutes, and some revisions were made to other white boarded comments. The room was full of smiles.

Sam leaned over to Philip and whispered, "What just happened?"

"We want everyone in the room to know they have value," Philip replied. "Later this week you will be learning that no idea is without merit. You just got a glimpse of how powerful that statement can be. You will note the group took time to briefly discuss what was brought up. It broke the stalemate they were in, and the person feels good about being part of the group. When you diminish no one you will see things move quickly, easily and peaceably."

Carol, Philip and Sam left the room a short time later. "What did you think?" asked Carol.

"I'm not sure what I saw in there," said Sam. "I know everyone sure had a lot of energy and while there was not yet agreement, you could almost feel the ideas beginning to gel around one concept so strongly as the way to go. Was there something else going on? I didn't get the sense there was the usual endless meeting taking place," replied Sam.

Philip spoke up, "It wasn't obvious to you, but in the corner of the room was a large sand-filled hourglass that was running. Each meeting room has a thirty minute, sixty minute, ninety minute and a two-hour hourglass. The movement of the sand is a visual reminder of the flow of time and our need to move along. Everyone in the room picked two hours for this meeting and agreed to move along thoughts and ideas to meet this deadline. The leader in the room was accepted and honored for keeping things going and acknowledging the time agreed upon to get it done."

"Our groups," interjected Carol, "understand that unlimited time meetings are just inviting things like conflict and low energy into the room. With these set times they can look at the progress they made in that time frame and portion out assignments. Then we do our research and reconvene later to be more effective. We know meetings are necessary, and we know people have limited attention spans and other things to do. If that group does not conclude today, they will meet again later in the day or tomorrow. The agenda will become tighter and tighter until the task is completed. The meetings will not get longer, nor will they be allowed too many more so everyone knows the best way to work is to 'Be involved and get it solved.'"

"Okay, I have to ask." said Sam, "What was with the moose ears?"

Carol and Philip laughed. "He was putting on his thinking cap," offered Carol.

"His thinking cap. That is the strangest thing I have ever heard," said Sam.

"Well you better get used to it because we all have them, even multiple sets of them," said Philip. "We use them to get our thought process going by creating smiles in the people around us and a smile in ourselves. You'll learn more about smiling on your day of smiling practice, and then it will make more sense."

Carol, Philip and Sam proceeded back to their original meeting room. Carol and Philip explained in detail, with illustrations, to Sam what "diminish no one" meant. They looked at newspaper headlines, clips from television shows and office videos on things not going right. They noted how each situation was handled without diminishing the other person. They also looked at how easily society accepts diminishment, even to the point of making sitcoms that use it for their entire premise. They discussed how small children start this behavior in the sandbox and then carry it into the schools and finally to their place of work. Carol and Philip talked earnestly about why and how this should not occur in their company. They showed that diminishing no one contributed to a better bottom line, in terms of profits and the making of a great place to work.

Sam's head was swimming as he followed Carol and Philip through the offices, the plant area and the shipping area. He noticed when something not very smart happened, managers and colleagues alike substituted their criticism with words of kindness in correcting the behavior. The energy of peace permeated even the toughest situations. Sam could tell that employees making mistakes were quick to pick up and correct their behavior, returning the honor received in words of kindness. What is this place, Sam thought. I feel like I am in an unreal world. Can people really spend an entire day diminishing no one? The thought went through Sam's head as they walked by the door to the employee parking lot. Sam noticed a sign over the door in large letters, *Thank You For Diminishing No One Today*. I guess my question is answered, thought Sam.

As the day ended Carol and Philip asked Sam to do some homework overnight. "When you are out in the world tonight, buying groceries, going to a movie, doing your laundry at the laundromat, practice this concept to see how easy it is. When there aren't any washers and you have to wait, don't diminish the people that got there first. When the line at the express is held up because the person can't find their wallet, don't diminish them in your mind by calling them names, just let them be, and diminish no one."

Sam left that evening thinking he may have just taken the hardest job of his life. And he hadn't even started his work! As he exited the building via the plant/employee exit he had been shown, he noticed a large reader board over the door running the comment, *Diminish No One*. How interesting, he thought. I guess they remind people of these things even after orientation.

2

Make No Judgment About Other's Choices

Sam smiled to himself as he entered the "Employee Entrance" the next morning. Once again he had parked in an "Employee of the Year" space and was beginning to get the feeling there was another story there yet to be told.

The employee entrance came directly into the manufacturing area of the company, which struck Sam as odd. He would have assumed that there were other entrances to offices, the call center and the like, but he had been told this was where he should report from now on. As he walked through the door he was greeted by two people who introduced themselves as Ted and Jan. Ted asked how he felt about what he had learned the first day. Sam readily admitted that it was all a bit confusing. He did notice from watching television sitcoms the night before that an abundance of diminishing comments were used for humor. He prodded Ted about the fact that this seems to be a readily accepted cultural norm on television. Ted responded that what they were trying to accomplish at their company often contradicted what was going on elsewhere in the world. Jan added that it was not what everyone else is doing, but what they feel is the right thing to do. Both Ted and Jan launched into a short and compelling story about the success of their company, through innovation, sales and marketing, and their ability to deal with the daily problems that was unmatched in other organizations.

Sam was once again struck by how enthused these people were

about their work and their organization. He followed Jan and Ted through the plant and then burst out laughing when he noticed that everyone in the plant had on silly socks, including Ted and Jan.

After his inquiring about this strange event, Ted apologized that Sam was not informed of silly sock day so he too could participate. He told Sam that the company likes to do things to make people laugh. Then to Sam's chagrin Ted pulled out the silliest pair of socks he had ever seen and handed them to Sam. The socks had different farm animals all over them and each animal had a name stenciled inside. The animals on the socks all had the names of the executives in the corporation. Ted explained that they were a gift and he could keep them. "Just in case you don't own silly socks, we wanted to be sure you were covered," piped in Jan.

They proceeded to the training room Sam had started in yesterday, and once again he was struck by the wonderful scents wafting through the building. Today's was peppermint. It made him smile and think of Christmas. Ted, noticing the smile, asked if it was because of the smell and Sam replied affirmatively. "We hope to stimulate your senses all day through smell, sound, visual effects and the occasional odd thing. We hope they make you laugh, keep up your energy and help you enjoy your work day," offered Ted. At that point Ted lifted his pant leg to display his multi-striped socks in neon orange, yellow and green. Sam began to worry that no one was ever serious at this organization.

Jan then introduced the topic for the day: *Make No Judgment About Other People's Choices*. Ted and Jan then launched into a funny dialogue about two people meeting on the beach and articulating what each was thinking rather than saying. The first person was assessing the second's clothes and thinking such things as "how can anyone think that shirt and those pants go together?" "Where on earth did he get that terrible haircut. It is right out of the sixties! He really needs to cut those sideburns shorter." The second person in turn was mentally assessing the first with such thoughts as "What a weird way she walks and can you believe she has on socks with her sandals on the beach?" "Why does she always choose to date such losers?" "She sure picks the wrong make-up for her face." Sam was laughing more and more as they upped the mental conversations to criticism about speech, boyfriends, jobs, etc. Eventually Jan and Ted turned to Sam and asked him if he thought the mental dialogue was real. Sam replied that while it was exaggerated a bit, quite a lot of it seemed possible when two people meet. Jan and Ted both smiled and welcomed him to the real world. They explained that it is both natural and normal to have judgments about what others are wearing, doing and saying.

They then went on to explain that at their company the employees were attempting to mitigate the negative effects that judging may have on working with one another. The example Jan brought up was commuting. When someone cuts you off in traffic or does something equally dangerous, we are quick to make a judgment about that person and the choice they have made. In making that judgment we then begin an internal process that is negative. We think they are bad, stupid, mean, crazy, offensive and more. Ted went on to explain that, in that moment, you can choose not to make a judgment about that person's choice and thus change your negative reaction or forestall it completely. In doing this, you create a different environment for yourself, for that person and for all those around you.

In the workplace this is most frequently seen in meetings and interactions about work. One person will bring in a report and others will immediately judge not only the report, but the layout, the research, the implications and so on. Jan pointed out that judgment versus analysis is at issue here. Were you to analyze what was done, you may find that the research is flawed, which is different than judging the research itself. Sam felt that Jan and Ted were splitting hairs and said so. Jan and Ted smiled and indicated that they were indeed doing just that. However, in that fine line was the difference between being able to hear and receive information for the good feedback that is in it and hearing and receiving information that is based on people perceiving the world differently than you do.

Jan suggested that they take a walk around the company to see this principle in action. Their first choice was the call center where they listened in on a complaining customer talking to an agent. The customer was ranting about the product they had received and the fact that it did not work as indicated. The responding agent spoke to the person in a calm, warm voice indicating they understood that what was happening was frustrating and that they would replace the product immediately at no charge to the customer. He closed the interaction by apologizing for the inconvenience and added that the customer would receive a coupon toward the purchase of future products for their trouble. The customer continued to harangue the agent until the final minutes, then finally agreed to receive the replacement and the gift. Sam was surprised to watch the agent take the next call with a smile in his voice and no signs of the conflict he had just been through.

Sam also noted that a few of the agents in the cubicles next to the agent handling the difficult call had stood up with hats on and blown bubbles toward him. One even flew over a small foam airplane.

Ted pointed out to Sam that the agent had been trained to make no judgment about the customer's choice to treat him rudely. The agent understood that the individual had a right to his behavior, and while he did not agree with it, he made no judgment about it, thus making the interaction easy for him. Jan explained that it is still difficult to take a call like that. So his co-workers were making him laugh and smile again to know that life was still good.

Sam spoke about how hard it would be for him not to judge someone who behaved so badly. "It is just what we do as human beings," he said. Jan and Ted agreed. They urged Sam to keep that thought as they moved to the next area of the company. A large meeting was taking place and the leader was explaining that he had made a decision. The decision was to open an office in a town that was hard to reach and without many major services that might be needed. Participants in the room were questioning the provisioning and travel costs relative to this choice. Sam watched in amazement while people prefaced their questions with, "I am not making a judgment about your choice. However, I need to understand why you think we can overcome this provisioning and transportation problem?" All the interactions were not only friendly, but exaggeratedly so. It was almost as if everyone was afraid to offend.

Sam asked about this, stating that confrontation and critiques were the essence of good business. Jan and Ted explained that that was an old norm they simply did not support. Confrontation is a negative interaction, analysis and explanation are positive interactions, and that is what we are all about was their reply. Critiques are negatives. Offering suggestions, adding on to what has already been said is positive. Asking for answers is positive, while stating that something doesn't make sense is negative. We make no judgment about the choice. We do ask to understand how and why it transpired.

Ted continued. "Sometimes people are in a position to make choices that fit what works for them. In this case the facility manager had worked hard to find a good workforce and an inexpensive place to build the new office. He had weighed this against the provisioning and travel costs and found it to be the best alternative. While people questioned his choice, they made no judgment about it. They also made it their business to get the facts before they discussed it too freely among themselves."

Jan and Ted pointed out that their company was based on trust. Part of that trust was that this facility manager would not go out and do something without doing his homework first. It was also part of this whole process that if he had somehow managed to overlook something big in his decision, he would be able to reverse himself without an adverse affect on the company. This was another aspect of making no judgment. He would not judge his own decision to be final until he gave his peers and other important persons, or all the people in the company, a chance to ask questions and help him make the best decision possible.

Sam mulled through his head this odd concept as he, Jan and Ted headed out for lunch. Finally he spoke up and asked why and how this came to be so important in the organization. Ted told him that their research of good places to work that turned a steady profit were almost always founded on this principle. It allowed people to enjoy freedom from worrying about whether their bow tie would keep them from getting a promotion. It gave them the insight to understand that judging without the facts in a situation was what created a negative workplace. Companies and employees who want to enjoy their work and accomplish good things found this principle allowed them to question freely. It did away with the petty and devastating comments that often pervade the workplace. Jan asked Sam if he could imagine a workplace where people knew for sure that no one would judge their choices, but would instead insist upon a questioning dialogue until all was understood.

Jan then spoke up, "Be clear that outcomes must eventually be judged. What we are proposing here is that you make no judgment about the path to get to that outcome. For example, people are different and often use different methods to achieve the same results. Someone may choose to drive from New York to Chicago, someone else fly and yet a third person takes the train. As long as they are there on time for what they need to attend to we should not judge their choice of transportation. In business too often a manager will decree how a project should be done versus allowing an employee to define their own method, which will still achieve an acceptable result. You probably know this as micromanagement. It is something we try hard to avoid using our 'no judgment' philosophy."

During lunch Ted and Jan pointed around the restaurant and asked Sam if he was able to suspend judgment about some of the choices that were being made by the people there. The woman who let her children run wild, the teen group that was talking louder than necessary, the gentleman that spoke into his cell phone like it was a speaker phone. All of these things are out of your control. Therefore, there is no reason for you to judge. It is their lives and their situation. Make your own a good one and ignore what others are doing. It only spoils your mood and ruins your clear thinking. Let them be.

Later in the day Jan and Ted sat with Sam and allowed him to ask more questions. Ted offered some further explanation on this subject via the author, Alan Cohen, and his book, *A Deep Breath of Life*. Ted pointed out that Alan discusses judgment versus discernment. In the book he states, "While we must not judge, we must discern. Judgment is distinguished by turbulent emotion and fear, while discernment is based on clarity and peace."

"And peace in our work is what we are after," finished Jan.

Jan and Ted spent the afternoon walking Sam through several other meetings and interactions where Sam repeatedly saw people checking their judgment. It was after all a natural response, almost an ingrained response. What he saw when they checked themselves was smiles, questions and exchanges that brought respect to every interaction. Sam was amazed it really worked.

When Sam combined this with what he had learned yesterday, 'diminish no one', he could see how logically these two concepts fell into place. If I do not want to diminish you then I make no judgment about your choice. I do retain the right to ask questions with respect, and you will take this information into consideration to make the best decision possible. Wow! This could really be a fun way to work.

As Sam walked out the employee exit that evening he noticed the reader board running his lesson for the day. Were they doing this just for him or do they do this all the time? Either way the board read, *Make No Judgement About Other Peoples Choices*.

3

Health of Body, Mind and Spirit (and Don't Forget to Play)

Sam began his third day with some trepidation. He wasn't sure that he could possibly get through an entire day without diminishing anyone, nor was he easily able to suspend judgment about other's choices. It just seemed so natural to do so. He was however committed to trying this new way of thinking and working.

Once again as he entered through the plant it seemed strange to him that all employees would come through that way. He needed to remember to ask about it. Again he was immediately distracted by the rock-and-roll music playing loudly and the laughter among the workers on the floor. One older lady approached him and introduced herself as Sharon, his guide for the day. She said they were going to begin the day all over again by going back out to his car. Sam was completely befuddled by this and followed meekly as she headed back out the door. Sharon turned as she got outside and asked Sam what he had done to prepare himself for coming to work that day. Sam could not for the life of him figure out what she meant. After a moment of silence, he asked if she meant if he took a shower. Sharon laughed and said while that always helped that wasn't exactly what she meant.

Sharon asked what he had done to mentally prepare himself to work for the company that day, to make sure he personally had a good day and to put a smile on his face and in his heart. Sam was puzzled over what all this really had to do with this work. However, he knew that things usually made sense after a while and decided he could begin to think about this. He told Sharon that he probably did the usual things in the morning, brush his teeth, take a shower, eat breakfast, get dressed and drive to work. He had never really thought consciously about what he was doing to prepare himself mentally for the day.

Sharon asked him to show her his car and Sam complied. They opened the door, peered inside and asked him if this was the way it always looked. Sam, thinking he had left spilled fast food or junk on the floor, peeked inside and noticed everything to be in order and proudly announced, that yes, he was always neat and clean with his car. Sharon then explained that she was actually referring to the fact that the car seemed to have none of Sam's personality.

Sam was confused. "What is a car personality?"

Sharon said, "I assume your home has pictures, paintings, collections of things you like and things that express who you are and make you feel good and at home."

Sam replied that he did in fact collect concert posters which were prominently displayed throughout his apartment. He also collected music and trains. Sharon asked him why none of this was reflected in his car. Sam, thoroughly confused on what this could possibly have to do with work, simply replied that it never occurred to him to do so.

Sharon then asked him to follow her inside where she would explain further what this was all about. In a brightly lit room with a small garden Sharon showed Sam some unusual items. The first was a large stuffed elephant, the next was a big laughing brown bear and the next a huge tiger with a great big grin on his face. Sharon explained that these were examples of "car partners," something to ride along in your passenger seat as quiet yet playful traveling companions.

"When you are riding along you can talk to them or just enjoy their grins. Check out the other cars in the parking lot," she encouraged, "you will see everything from big stuffed dogs to small bean bags on the dashboard to bobble headed creatures in the back window. We believe that commuting anywhere should be fun. I hope you have music you love or good radio stations that make you laugh available, too. Always carry bubbles in the console of your car and when you get stuck at a red light have some fun blowing them out the window. Carry a smiling face on a stick and wave it at people. Smile at others as you drive and when someone does something foolish, as they are known to do, make no judgment about their choice and go on to enjoy your day."

Sam was totally befuddled. What on earth did this have to do with his new job? Sharon smiled in amusement reading Sam's mind. "We believe that how you start your day before you get to work has a lot to do with how you will work once you get here. We have a morning routine that you might enjoy and want to try."

Sam was almost afraid to ask. Sharon sat across from him at the table and asked to see his smile. Now Sam was really worried. Did they honestly expect him to smile all the time? While Sam was a happy person he didn't go around grinning constantly. He was in fact a bit staid in that department. Sharon however persisted and he grinned, a little.

"Show me your teeth and really smile!" she laughed.

Sam did a big goofy smile and Sharon smiled in return. "Now do that smile every day before you ever leave your bed and watch how much better the world gets," she said.

Sam thought she was nuts. But it seemed like something he could try. Sharon then went on to explain that how he started the day and the attitude he gave himself would affect how he interacted with others, enjoyed his work and his day, and created what he wanted out of life. She suggested that he shower with a pig or a frog or a lobster that would lift his mood. At this point Sam was sure she was joking. Until she showed him a shower pal that was shaped just like the animals she mentioned.

"I am not trying to make you do anything but think about good things in your shower," Sharon continued. "Preplan your day to be a success and a joyful experience. Ask the world to deliver good things to you and for you to do well at all you attempt. Ask for patience for the flat tires, spilled coffee and late reports that will inevitably come. Use this preparation time in the morning to pump up your energy, laugh, even dance and sing, if it is in your nature. Prepare to have a good day and then watch it magically unfold in front of you."

"Enjoy your commute and look for fun things along the way. Find signs that make no sense or make you laugh. Wave at people along the way to work. Sing or talk to yourself and get the ideas flowing for all you hope to accomplish that day.

I know this seems inane to you, but trust me. It all works and it works well." Sharon continued. "There has even been a study done that correlates the negative interaction of employees in the first two hours of work to things that happened during their commute that made them upset or angry. Don't let this happen to you. Don't bring it into the workplace, is what we are hoping our employee's will hear," finished Sharon.

Sharon then led Sam out of the room while explaining that the company was firmly committed to healthy living and lifestyles. "This means different things for people, so I will show you some of the options we have built into our environment for you."

Their first stop was at a door marked "**Body.**" Inside was a small workout area with a treadmill, stair-stepping machine, stationary bike and a locker room with showers and weights.

"This room is used to help us keep our bodies going. We also have a walking and jogging trail outlined in and around the office park. Employees are encouraged to use this before, during and after work as it works best for them. They can also have access to this on the weekends and late into the evening. You will note that it has a special door to the outside for these after-hours visits. People are all different and do things at different times to meet their personal needs, and we respect that. What is most important is that people take care of themselves. We field co-ed softball, bowling, basketball and volleyball teams as well and you are welcome to join one of them."

Sharon then took him on a quick tour of the company cafeteria. Sam immediately noticed some things were in machines with the usual charges while others were free. It didn't take long to notice that the chips and candy cost money while the fruit and energy bars were free. Sharon said it was company policy to provide free healthy snacks to all employees. It was an honor system and they didn't find things "going home," but simply consumed in the workplace as it was meant. Fridays feature free popcorn and Mondays featured free doughnuts. She laughed as Sam's eyebrows shot up in surprise.

"We aren't completely off the wall. Some days you just need a doughnut and Monday seemed like a good day for that treat," she explained.

Their next stop was a complete surprise to Sam. The door they were entering was simply labeled "**Mind**." They then walked into a beautifully decorated library with books, computers and magazines juxtaposed to lounge chairs, couches, tables and reading lamps. Several people were in the room reading and others on the computers.

"Why would they use the computer here if everyone has one on their desk?" asked Sam.

"Well, first of all not everyone has access to a personal computer," said Sharon. "As you will recall there are no computers for personal use in the plant area or in the call center. This gives our employees a chance to have email at work as some do not have computers at home, or to do personal searches on the web on their breaks or lunch hours, or before and after work. We know people in the offices often use the internet for personal searches and we simply ask that they do them away from the work area to avoid the conflict of time for personal business and the time for work. So they come in here. We also have easy on-line benefits enrollments and changes as well as company information on-line. We release people on work time to check these things out and get them done as needed."

Sam should have been prepared for their next stop but wasn't. The door said "**Spirit**." Sharon could tell Sam wasn't sure he wanted to go in this room and was already making plans not to use it. Surprisingly enough the room was completely matted with a soft light blue mat. There were large green plants in the corners, a mirrored wall and a few cushioned chairs next to a small waterfall in one corner. Sharon showed Sam a schedule for yoga and Tai Chi classes that were offered, again in the early morning, over the lunch hours and in the evening. She explained that the room was also open all day for "quiet space" as people needed it. No talking and no shoes were the two rules posted. One of the walls had a door to a small meditation garden with benches, another waterfall and beautiful flowers in abundance. Sharon explained that the employees actually did the gardening on a volunteer basis and Sam noticed small name plates next to different sections of the garden. In the corner sat a sandbox with shovels, pails and trucks and Sam could see that someone had built a sand castle. Sam asked if children used the area. Sharon explained that the castle had actually been built by an employee taking a "play break" while working on an extremely difficult project.

"We have discovered that we need to play when things get really tight or tense around here," Sharon explained. "It opens our minds, relaxes our bodies and creates new energy that leads to solutions and new ideas. You might see someone walking around with their thinking cap on to get playful and get people to engage them in a way that will re-energize them. You might see the bubbles, like in the call center yesterday, or they might just go to the playroom."

The playroom, thought Sam. This I have to see. Once again reading his thoughts Sharon led him to a door marked "**The Playroom**."

Sam could never have prepared himself for what he saw next. The room was right out of grade school. There were pipe cleaners, clay, paints, paper, crayons, beach balls, Nerf balls, plastic golf clubs and balls and much, much more. Brightly decorated kites hung from the ceiling. At the moment they walked in two men were engaged in a lively conversation with their hands in finger paints and elaborate drawings all around them. They seemed so intent on their play or work, whatever it was, they didn't even notice the new arrivals.

"What you see is what it is," Sharon said. "We dedicated this space to the fact that sometimes we just need to play to get unstuck, to get our energy up and to get going again. We have had people come in here and play after a tragedy to remind them that life is joyful. We have people doing what these two are doing now, working out a problem with their hands because their minds won't cooperate at the moment. A group may even do a meeting in here if the issue is sticky and people want to keep up the energy. Would you like to try one of the pinball machines? They are a lot of fun and can really work out negative energy."

Sam smiled as he stepped over to an old fashioned pinball machine and gave it a whirl. This is too much fun. It can't be true. What is with these people, he thought?

Sharon finished their day together by explaining how critical the whole person was to the company. "We expect you to do good work here, and often that is hard work. We know you have energy ups and downs, and we know that other things in your life will impact how you are feeling. These four rooms are designed to help you take care of your health, feed your mind, nurture your spirit and keep the playfulness in your heart. With these in sync you have a better chance of success at your work. Even if we didn't offer special spaces for these activities you could build them into your office by putting good reading on your bookshelf, taking a walk during your break, doing meditation during the day to relax for a few minutes, and putting some fun, playful items in your desk drawer. Maybe even blowing a bubble now and then!"

Sam thanked Sharon for the delightful and very different day. As he headed back through the plant to the employee exit, he noticed the reader board once again reflected his orientation with a reminder running that said, *Take care of body, mind and spirit; and don't forget to **play**!*

4

No Idea Is Without Merit

The day dawned crisp and clear as Sam headed to work humming along with his favorite CD playing in his car after the encouragement from Sharon yesterday. Sam could not help but notice the difference in his attitude, as he did wake up and smile and really planned to have a great day. He smiled to himself while he pondered what silent partner would make it to his front seat. Godzilla seemed his style. He was however, going to reserve judgment for a few days.

Entering the plant Sam smelled the scent of fresh apple pie, and his mouth began to water despite the good hearty breakfast. Two gentlemen approached and introduced themselves to him as Jack and Aaron. Jack explained they would be going right into a meeting on a new project that Sam would eventually be working on. It involved new products, new methods of distribution and an unusual advertising campaign. Sam was excited to finally get down to the meat of his work. He worried briefly that he had no idea what they were working on or going to be talking about and hoped he would be able to just listen in this first meeting.

The meeting room Sam, Jack and Aaron entered was gaily decorated and a buffet of fruit, juices and energy bars lined one side of the room. The participants ranged from the CEO to people from the plant and many more. A gentleman stood and called the meeting to order with a bicycle horn. Everyone grabbed a seat, and silence came over the room. The gentleman introduced himself as Michael, the Vice President for

Sales and Marketing. He looked directly at Sam and welcomed him to the company on behalf of all the employees. He then asked each person in the room to stand and introduce themselves to Sam with their name, area of responsibility and their expectation for this meeting. Sam proceeded to hear expectations that ranged from a solid marketing plan to understanding more about the product to people looking for answers on how this new ad campaign would work and what they could do to help.

An agenda was handed to each person, and the expectations Sam had just heard were neatly typed next to each item. Obviously the question had been asked before. A very quick glance showed his name as a participant with no expectation next to it which gave him great relief. Michael then spoke directly to Sam and asked him to be prepared to enter an expectation about one hour into the meeting. Sam was totally befuddled as to what that might be. However, he nodded in agreement.

The meeting started with an overview of the product and its design. Questions rang around the room while the product development people explained what was what. After everyone was polled to see if they understood how it worked, they then moved on to the distribution. Michael explained that it was going into stores that had not previously carried their products. This raised many questions ranging from the viability studies that were done to volumes that were anticipated.

Sam noted that he heard the plant personnel doing a great deal of questioning and participation during the sales presentation. This pleased him, as their questions were very much from the consumer perspective and added quite a bit of spice to the meeting.

A break was called, and Jack and Aaron pulled Sam aside to talk. Jack asked what Sam had observed, and he responded on his observation about the plant personnel. Jack smiled and asked if there was any thing else he had observed. Sam thought hard but nothing came to mind. Jack asked if he had heard the word "but" in the meeting so far. Sam replied that while he listened closely, he couldn't say if he had or had not. "Why," he asked?

"Well your lesson for today is that this company believes that no idea is without merit. You heard this before, whenever groups or even two people meet to talk we try to avoid the word 'but' and use 'or' or 'and' to build on the thought put out on the table. In this way we honor each idea that comes forth and the person that offered the thought, even if it is off the wall in our opinion." Before he could say more Michael returned to the room and reconvened the meeting.

Michael called on Sam to share with the group what his expectation was, Sam paled as he realized he had not put anything down on his paper. Pausing for a moment, Sam suddenly brightened and said to the group, "My expectation from this meeting is to understand more about the concept that no idea is without merit."

The room burst into applause as Sam beamed. Michael then called upon the group to really up the ante on ideas in this segment to reinforce the learning for Sam and to help the advertising group come up with a good campaign.

You could feel the excitement in the room as the ad group led a lively discussion about the best way to announce and market the product. Sam was stunned at some of the ridiculous things that were tossed out and how people parleyed these ideas into things that were usable. At one point when things began to bog down, out came the huge colored beach balls Sam had seen before and they began tossing them around the room. As people caught the balls they found themselves blurting out ideas which were being recorded on white boards around the room. The CEO never condemned an idea or even reacted to outrageous ones, rather participated and added thoughts along with others. Sam had almost forgotten she was the CEO in the midst of all the conversation. Deference was given to all participants equally and Sam noted the concept of "no idea is without merit" again and again.

In a very short time a powerful ad campaign was formed, minus the details. Everyone agreed that they were on the way. The ad group thanked everyone and promised focus group feedback from outside consumers in a very short time.

Sam was amazed. They had accomplished more in two hours than he had seen groups do in a month of meetings. How did that happen? Sam posed the question to Jack and Aaron.

"We know that meetings can be useful only if we are clear on the outcomes, clear on group expectations and stay on the topic, Aaron responded. "You will notice that no one in the room went off on a tangent, brought in other issues or dishonored another regardless of what they thought. I promise you that many notes were taken by people on the tangential issues that came up in their minds. They will then take these thoughts to the appropriate parties outside of the meeting and get them taken care of."

Sam could not believe this was all happening so easily and asked if this was staged just for him. Jack laughed and said no, it really was the way they worked every day. Jack then motioned Sam to come along to view another way this idea worked in the organization.

The three men entered an area in the plant that was in the middle of the manufacturing area. It had a long table and chairs around it with two signs overhead that said "**Quality**" and "**Safety**." A group of people were engaged in a conversation when Jack asked if they could sit in and observe. The man leading the group assured them that was fine and once again introduced each person at the table to Sam. The conversation turned out to be about a machine that seemed to continually break down at critical times and the machine manufacturers, slow response to getting it fixed. The group reviewed a previous list of ideas that were generated around the problem and noted that they seemed to be on the right path. Yet problems continued.

Suddenly someone turned to Sam and asked what he thought they should do. Sam at first responded that he really had no idea. Jack and

Aaron both encouraged Sam to give it a try, since no idea is without merit. Sam thought for a moment and then asked about the service contract on the equipment. He was told that it was standard and required the manufacturer to complete the repair. Sam then asked if it could be renegotiated to include both incentives and penalties when the repair was needed.

"We never thought of that," replied one of the men and they busily began writing out what that contract would look like. While the problem was larger in that they didn't want the machine to break down at all, this was a way to get more attention until the larger problem was resolved.

Sam left the plant with Jack and Aaron feeling oddly thrilled that he was able to make a contribution.

As Sam, Jack and Aaron sat together Aaron explained that not every idea is perfect or can be implemented. However, using the concept of "no idea is without merit," they are able to get people to speak up and keep talking until things get done.

"When we use this concept we are not trying to say that every idea should be implemented and used. We are saying that they have merit in their own way and as part of a larger overall plan for the company," added Jack.

Sam laughed and said, " I guess if everyone said I have an idea that we should all get raises, it might create quite a stir, and I can see how it wouldn't be easily implemented."

"True," replied Jack. "However the idea would be probed for why it came up and what was behind the thought. Did the individual feel they were paid inadequately for their responsibilities? Was there a real or perceived unfairness? And so on and so on. You see, no idea is without merit."

Sam spent the remainder of the day in smaller interactions while people worked out problems, created new ideas and made plans for how things would be done. He saw again and again that one idea led to another, and the use of the word "but" was missing most of the time.

People listened and added thought to thought creating spectacular results.

As Sam headed home for the day he waved to his new friends in the plant and noticed once again that the reader board over the exit read, *No Idea Is Without Merit.*

5

Trust is a Given

The rainy day didn't dampen Sam's mood as he pulled into his "Employee of the Year" parking spot. He always got a kick out of that painted saying, and it stimulated his thinking about what an employee of the year really was.

As he entered the building, a woman stepped up and introduced herself to Sam as Beth. She asked him if he enjoyed the rain as much as she did, and they proceeded to share stories about jumping in puddles as children and listening to the rain while reading a good book.

They proceeded into the office area and she pointed to a brightly lit office with Sam's name and job description on the outer wall.

"We thought it was time for you to see your office and where you will be working," said Beth. "I know we have run you all over the building this week and we appreciate that you have done so without ever asking where you will work. It shows that you are concerned about the company and what you have to give versus where you will work. That is important, because we are all really here to accomplish something together."

Sam looked around his new workspace and found it to be very comfortable and pleasant. He could see his co-workers through the glass walls. Beth showed him a knob that turned the clear glass to smoky glass creating privacy when it might be needed. Sam also saw a stream that he remembered from the lobby coming through the center of the building. There were many plants and even some water fountains as part of the interior. All in all, it was warm, pleasant and definitely more peaceful than anywhere he had worked before. Beth explained the computer system, his passwords and email and the various company directories and files that could be accessed. Sam was surprised at the amount of access he had and mentioned that to Beth. She smiled and explained that he had just stumbled across his lesson for the day, "trust is a given." Beth talked about the fact that employees in the company needed to know they would and could be trusted with as much information as possible. She explained that monthly financials were available on-line, along with much, much more. She also told Sam that people were encouraged to put their work in progress on-line and ask for comments from others. Sam was amazed, here he was practically a stranger, and yet he could read and see what would be considered by many as very confidential information.

Sam pressed Beth as to how this worked for the company. Concerns about the competition and others getting into this were the first things on his mind.

"First of all," said Beth, "we believe we are all here for the same reason: to make this company successful and make ourselves successful at the same time. That means we get to do good work, get paid well for it, and share in the success of the things we create. In order for all those things to be possible we must trust each other all the time. We do have a level of security for entry into the building that is just common sense. However, once you are cleared to be in this building we consider you part of our team, and therefore we trust you." Beth smiled at Sam and said, "It shows from the simple things to the critical things we do."

They left Sam's office and headed for the employee cafeteria. Beth explained that trust in an organization started with something as simple as lunch. Opening one of several refrigerators supplied to the employees Sam noted the labeled lunch bags and boxes.

"In our company we know our lunch will be here," offered Beth.

"As simple as that sounds, it is one of the ways that you know you are working in a trustworthy environment. No one would ever consider taking property that is not theirs. Likewise, we trust people to clean up after themselves," and she pointed to the pristine cafeteria area. "We share this space and trust each other to honor that."

"At a higher level you have seen the access to information on our systems," offered Beth. "It is with this information that people can see and know how to make informed decisions about their work and about how to offer help to others. As you learned earlier in the week, we do not diminish one another, make judgments about their choices or ever dismiss ideas offered. All of these things require a level of trust that goes beyond the norm. To help us know and understand what will happen all day here, trust must be a given."

"Let me show you some simple ways this plays out every day at work," said Beth. They walked into the mailroom area which was a beehive of activity. Sam noted a counter area marked incoming and another marked outgoing and boxes and sorting trays throughout the area. In addition, there were the usual postage machines, weighing machines and envelopes for various overnight and two-day delivery companies. Nothing too unusual here, thought Sam. As if reading his thoughts Beth commented on the fact that when you brought something to this group to be delivered elsewhere, anywhere in the world you trusted that it would arrive safely and on time.

"99% of the time that is true," she noted. "Occasionally there is a misstep, but not very often. This is an example of where trust is a given. You actually practice it every day, a million times a day without even thinking."

Beth pointed out examples outside of work such as buying and eating food you trusted as safe or driving your car and being safe on the roads. "Trust is really a given in so much that we do," Beth concluded. "Now what we have to do, is take that same level of trust into the workplace. We have to believe and know that everyone is acting in the best interest of the company and for the good of all. This is a big step in a world where we have seen and know of people who have worked for personal gain to the detriment of the company and others in the company."

Sam asked how you make this quantum leap to total trust when you don't even know the other people involved.

"Good question," replied Beth. "One of the things you do is to make sure that you do know the other people involved. If you will notice on our intranet we have listed a photo, name, job description and a commitment statement for each employee. We make a point of knowing each other in big and small ways. That is why the company extracurricular activities are really encouraged: sports, charity events and community service. We also look for people to volunteer on internal committees such as safety, quality, compensation and fun."

"Whoa, said Sam, "you have an employee compensation committee? Isn't that dangerous?"

"Not in an environment of trust," replied Beth. "We know that there is value to work and that that value will vary based on the contributions people make. Employees contribute their special skills and talents and so much more. We have a committee that assists our People and Work Department to do the best we can for all concerned and in the best interests of the organization. We pay well but are by no means the highest paying employer in the area. People know how their pay is determined and trust that they have received full value for what they bring to the table and contribute. We review salaries yearly on the employee's anniversary date and discuss how they are being paid in detail. Raises are not a given here, but can be earned based on an increasing contribution to the organization. We honor loyalty, but do not feel it is an automatic reason for a pay increase. Work is the reason for pay, and the better people are at their work, the more they can contribute and the more we will pay them."

Sam's head was reeling as he took all of this in. Was this a good
thing? He wasn't quite sure and could not wait to talk to more people
about their compensation experience over time.

Beth walked Sam back to his office where he was introduced to
Patrick, his new boss. Beth excused herself and said she would see him
again in a few minutes. Patrick sat down with Sam and walked him
through the structure of the department and a rough outline of some of
the first things Sam would be asked to work on. Patrick then shared a
little about himself, his family and hobbies. He told Sam he had been
there for about five years and found it to be one of the most enjoyable
experiences he had ever had. Patrick said work and play had begun to
blur in his mind, as he enjoyed the time at work so much. He cautioned
Sam that although it was a lot of fun and there was much to do, it was
still important for Sam to have a life outside the office. He asked Sam
if there were any hobbies or special interests he had. Sam proceeded to
speak about his love of skiing, hiking and collecting music.

At this point Patrick pointed out some features of Sam's office that
he had originally overlooked when he was meeting with Beth. First he
had already been provisioned with paper, pens, notes, stapler and other
items. Next he had a key on his phone that rang directly in Patrick's
office, sort of a super speed dial. Patrick explained that while they did
not work side by side, he wanted all his staff to know they could access
him quickly, if need be. He asked that it be used judiciously, and Sam
readily agreed.

Patrick then invited Sam to join him in meeting the other people
in his unit. They walked to one of the meeting rooms where a large
banner had been hung, saying "Welcome Sam." About ten people were
gathered there, and each had a gift for Sam. As they went around the
room, they introduced themselves with details similar to the conversation
Sam had just had with Patrick. He found out names, job descriptions,
commitments and some fun side things about families and interests

outside the workplace. As each one finished they handed Sam their present.

"Open it," they shouted and Sam complied. The first one was a ruler that was inscribed, "I trust you." As they continued around the room Sam received other office items with the same description. Patrick was the last to hand him a gift. It was a tee shirt with "I trust you" on the front and "You can trust me" inscribed on the back. He grasped Sam's hand, gave him a firm handshake and looked him in the eye.

"We have an important job here and that is to trust one another beyond what you have experienced before. I hope you will join us," he announced. Sam was awed to silence. Can trust be a given?

As Sam left the meeting he walked companion-like along side Patrick and asked a question that had been plaguing him for several days. Sam asked Patrick why it was on his fifth day of joining the company that he was finally meeting his boss, seeing his office and meeting his departmental colleagues. Patrick smiled sheepishly. After stopping in the hallway and facing Sam, Patrick explained that the concepts that Sam had been learning over the past four days were so critical to the organization that people were immersed in them and watched to see if they would be able to accept them and work by them. New employees were observed to see if they would become argumentative about the principles, or make fun of the concepts of body, mind, spirit and play or any other signs that these principles were just not a match for the new employee. Sam took in all of what Patrick had said and replied that he had worked with people who would do just that. "What if I had, too?" asked Sam.

Patrick explained that they had a meticulous hiring process and were accurate in picking people who would accept and practice these workplace principles about 98% of the time.

"If we make a mistake, which is about 2% of the time, we move quickly to see if remedial intervention will help or we have to help the person find another position," Patrick explained.

Sam was shocked by this thought and Patrick noticed his expression.

"Understand," replied Patrick, "if we let even one person in the organization be diminishing, make judgments about choices, show a lack of trust, or tell someone their idea has no merit, and then we are setting ourselves up for everyone to fall back into these behaviors. I know it is hard to imagine working with these principles all the time, but after a while they become second nature."

Sam left for the weekend under the reader sign that said simply, *I trust you.*

6

Unexpected Outcomes Bring Lessons

The rain of the past week had cleared, giving way to a bright and sunny day as Sam drove to work to begin his second week. Over the weekend he had spotted an action figure of one of his favorite heroes in a store window. This action figure was now riding beside him in the passenger seat helping defeat bad guys all the way to work. Sam's travel companion sparked Sam's smile, and he understood more about making his car a fun place to be. It really lifted his mood.

As Sam pulled into the parking lot, he marveled at how firmly he was already committed to this organization, although he had not even begun to do "real" work. Sam thought about how this commitment seemed to come from a sense that he would be treated well, not just by his boss, but by all the people he would work with and around. He also planned to be more tolerant of others, using all the principles he had been learning.

He was greeted as he entered by Patrick, his new boss, and they went directly to Patrick's office. Patrick showed Sam a wall of documents, photos and other items that all had red markings on them indicating some type of problem. Patrick explained that these were unexpected outcomes, or in other words, mistakes they had made along the way. Sam laughed and said with the attention you all have to doing the right thing, I am surprised this ever happens.

Patrick laughed with Sam and said, "Life is definitely not perfect, even here. We do have a principle that applies to these errors that you need to learn quickly and integrate into your work. Unexpected outcomes are always deeply probed for the lessons they bring. The world has learned many great things from failures, and the world has failed to learn from their mistakes, too."

Patrick then went on to give several examples from history of enormous failures that led to great discoveries and, in the long run, better outcomes. He asked Sam to think of a few times in his work life and his personal life when things had gone awry, he had made a mistake or something tragic had occurred.

"Ponder these things, if you will, and tell me one or two and the lessons you think you have learned from them."

Sam began to think and was embarrassed to mention a few. Besides he couldn't think of one good thing that had come out of them.

"Don't be afraid," encouraged Patrick. "Take some time to really think about this. The process of trial and error is literally a foundation for discovery. How would the polio vaccine, nuclear fission and so much more have occurred if people were not willing to try and try again? Also, what if they were not willing to look at what didn't work and analyze it in great detail to figure out how to get it right? All the work that had gone before would be wasted."

"One thing that you need to know and learn to grow with our company," said Patrick, "is that the ability to move forward, progress and succeed both individually and as an organization requires that we learn and learn big time from our mistakes."

Sam's head was swimming. He was so used to be cautious about making mistakes, fixing mistakes and sometimes even covering up mistakes that he wasn't sure how to respond. It seemed to make sense that we had something to learn, but why was this such a big issue? Sam finally decided to just ask the question. Patrick responded amiably that the company had a motto that each failure was a new piece in building what was needed to succeed. These pieces were to be honored for the gift or lesson that they bring to building a strong company.

"Of course we move quickly to fix our mistakes," said Patrick. "And of course we are cautious to do our homework and try not to make mistakes to begin with, but you know that things will happen. Often things happen that, with all the planning in the world, you just could not see or avoid. Weather is a good example. If a snowstorm shuts down a supplier, and we cannot make a deadline we have to deal with it. Illness or accidents come in the same category. Sometimes information from a source outside the organization is inaccurate. Each time we get the opportunity, we learn from what has happened."

"Now back to you, Sam," said Patrick. "Did you think of something that had happened and what you learned?"

Sam was slow to reply but decided that his new boss was someone he could trust, because, after all, "Trust is a given." Sam related a story about how he had worked night and day on a project at his last company to the point of exhaustion. When the time came to present the project plan to his boss and colleagues, he realized he left out a small but critical part of the plan and underestimated the project costs. Sam could still feel the humiliation of being called on this in the meeting and the berating he received later from his boss behind closed doors.

"Well that is a pretty big admission," said Patrick. "Now tell me what you learned from that."

Sam paused and then said, "Well, I really never spent much time looking at what I had learned, I was so busy fixing the mistake and trying never to do it again."

Patrick suggested that they take the time right then to walk through the situation and see how it happened. They went over how Sam had planned the project, what outline and forms he had used as guides, where he went to get help from others and where he did not. They looked at what his life and work schedule were at the time and what Sam was doing to keep himself not only focused but relaxed, so clear thinking could come through. When the two of them finished this in-depth review of everything that had transpired, Sam had a long list of things he had learned. Patrick seemed inordinately pleased which really confused Sam.

"Knowing that I had this much to learn and made so many mistakes, how can you possibly have confidence in me?" asked Sam, "Easy," said Patrick. "Look how quickly and thoroughly you were able to see what you did, where you could change it and what you missed. You have the gift of self esteem, knowing you are a good person. Coupled with that gift you have the gift of introspection. You can look at what you have done, ponder what occurred, see how you could have done it differently and move on. That one piece, moving on, is more important than anything," Patrick added. "People can become paralyzed by fear after an unexpected outcome or mistake, and then they are useless to themselves and the company. When bad things happen, deal with them, fix them. Thoroughly analyze these difficult situations for the lessons they bring and move on to bigger and better days."

Sam sat back amazed. Is this possible, he thought? Patrick went on to say that completing a "lesson plan" in their company was as important as fixing the mistake.

"If we just run around trying to fix the problem, and don't spend the time to look at the lessons we needed to learn, we will crawl up the mountain of success rather than race up."

Patrick went over to the wall they looked at when they first came in the room. He pointed to a specific page and looked back at Sam.

"This is one of my lessons that I have never forgotten," said Patrick. "When I was working on this I put everything I had into it, late nights, weekends, endless research and questioning. I was going to get this perfect if it killed me in the process, and it almost did."

Patrick paused and looked out the window of his office to the water flowing by in the indoor stream. "We are like that water," he said. "We need to flow with things, not fight with them. I was fighting everything and everyone to make this perfect, when what I needed to do most of all was go with the flow. Not just the flow of the work, but with my life, too. I was so focused on perfection that other things slid, and I missed things because I was tired and burnt out. I didn't have clear thinking and made a monumental error in judgment on one small piece that almost ruined the entire thing. I learned to pace myself. I learned to ask for more help and not try to do everything by myself. I learned that I don't know everything, and I learned that taking a break from things and relaxing, playing, resting and coming back with fresh eyes had more to offer than I understood at that time."

Patrick related to Sam the story of Mozart composing one of his most famous concertos over a game of billiards and Charles Dickens getting all the inspiration for *A Christmas Carol* walking around London after he found he could not write. "These are lessons for us," he said. "We need not to always go after things with a vengeance, but rather with a nap."

Patrick and Sam spent the rest of the day together while Patrick outlined in detail what Sam would be working on in the coming weeks. During frequent breaks from going through this work, Patrick took Sam to visit with the CEO and several of Sam's colleagues. Each one was asked by Patrick to relate an unexpected outcome they had had personally and what they had learned. Each person complied with a lively story that contained the incident, the fix and the lessons learned. Sam heard things from forgetting to lock up the building and a subsequent theft to missing out on a big contract. In every case, the person spoke clearly about what had occurred and their role in it and then spoke about the lessons they had learned from the situation. The expression "learn from your mistakes" was ringing in his ears at the end of the day.

Late in the day a colleague stopped by Sam's office and asked if he would like to come along that evening to a company softball game. Sam said he would definitely like to come and watch, and they made plans to meet after work.

Sam left in time for his rendezvous for the game, noting the reader board over the door read, *We all make mistakes, but do we all learn from them?*

7

It's Not About the Money

The morning had gone along swiftly for Sam. He had enjoyed the company of several other employees who had stopped in to help him in his work. Being so new, he was not aware of the shortcuts they had quickly pointed out to him.

Around ten o'clock his phone rang. Pamela from the office of People and Work asked if he was available for a compensation meeting at eleven o'clock that day. Sam replied that he was. Pamela explained the meeting location and that other new employees from the plant, the call center, sales team and administration would be in attendance. She then apologized for the late invitation, saying his name had inadvertently been left off the list for the meeting that day.

"We made a mistake and we are looking for the lesson here so we don't repeat it. Meanwhile, I hope you will accept our apologies and be able to attend without too much disruption to your work."

Sam indicated that he was in a position to come. Pamela said they would be finished at one o'clock and that lunch would be provided.

Sam settled into his seat promptly at eleven o'clock and noted that as always everyone showed up on time. Not once since he had joined the company had meetings been delayed waiting for people, and no one had shown up late. Sam knew immediately that this was another principle. He began to understand that some really basic things indicated the respect that was mentioned when he walked in the door the very first day. Being on time is a sign of respect for the people you work with, despite the many demands on your time. He knew that time management would be a sign of respect. He made a mental note not to show up late when a meeting was planned in advance. He knew that it was his responsibility to manage his schedule and be where he should be at all times.

Once again, as in all other meetings, introductions were made as well as explanations of positions and commitments. Now having a good handle on what he should be accomplishing, Sam was able to speak for the first time about his commitment. It felt very good.

Pamela put a large matrix up on the screen for everyone to view. Across the top of the matrix were all the different divisions of the company. The departments represented were Administration, Information Technology, Plant, Call Center, Sales, Marketing and more. Down the left side were the job titles for the company. Pamela showed how you could put your finger on a job title in the left hand column then go across to the department where that job was, and in the corresponding box find the salary range for that position. Sam was stunned. He could find the current range for his salary, the salary of the CEO and the salary ranges for all the other people in the company. Trust was once again being shown through openness about how people were paid.

Pamela then pointed to a percentage figure in the bottom right hand corner of each salary box. This was the bonus percentage that each employee was eligible for each year. Bonuses were paid on a quarterly basis, so you could receive up to one-fourth of the amount each quarter. Sam noted immediately, as did all the others in the room, that the lowest percentage amount was 5 percent of annual salary and the highest 20 percent. The percentages worked up from 5 percent to 20 percent, using almost every number in between.

Next she showed how the bonus was determined. This was getting very interesting. Pamela showed a three tiered review that determined the quarterly bonus. The first review was at the corporate review level.

"First, the company must meet its objectives for the quarter. These are usually in the major categories of customer satisfaction, quality and earnings, although they may be set differently in other quarters."

"In the next level of review the department would have a financial or accomplishment-based goal," Pamela continued. "For example, sales might have a financial target to make, the plant have a production target to make, the call center may have a quality target, and so on. The bonus amount carried forward from the corporate review level would then once again be awarded a certain percentage, depending on department performance."

"Finally, the last review was based on the individual's performance during that quarter. This is where it gets interesting." said Pamela. "If the company and departmental performances came in at 100 percent and you came in with an "A" level performance, you would receive the full bonus amount. If you came in at "B" you would only receive a 10 percent reduction from the amount carried down, and a "C" would be a 20 percent reduction. If you are graded below a "C" you do not receive any bonus, even if the company and department bonuses are in place. Should your manager rate you a "Star" for the quarter, you would be eligible for 110 percent of the bonus carried down. Each quarter we look for a few people who will fit into this category."

"As you can see," said Pamela, "We have to be doing things right on all three levels to be successful. Every department has to contribute to the overall success, we have to succeed in our departments and we have to succeed as individuals."

Next was the annual performance review process. This session explained that raises were given based on the level of competency shown in work performance and the individual's on-going contribution to the overall success of the organization.

"Increases are not based on length of service, but on performance and contribution," said Pamela. "We feel continued service makes people better at their work, and this quality of work is what we will reward."

Questions were then encouraged from the group. There were many. People asked if the bonus had not been paid in any recent quarters, and Pamela explained that it had not been paid twice in the last two years. This meant that bonuses were paid six out of eight possible times. People asked how the percentages were assigned to positions, and Pamela explained that they were done by level of impact which increased the success of the organization the most. The fact that every position was eligible for a bonus meant that everyone had something to give. Some people were in positions that had a greater impact, both good and bad, and thus they received potentially higher percentage bonus amounts.

At this point there was a rap on the door. Carrying pizzas, salads and cold drinks for the group were, amazingly enough, the CEO and three Vice Presidents of the organization. After everyone helped themselves to lunch Pamela continued the program with the executives remaining in the room.

Pamela then made a statement that Sam did not expect to hear in this meeting. "It's not about the money," she said. Everyone looked at her as if she was crazy. After all, that was just what they had been talking about for the past hour.

Pamela then went into a diagram that showed their company product from beginning to end. At the end was the satisfied customer with a big smile on their face and a happy outcome due to the products and services purchased.

"This is what it is all about," said Pamela. "If we do our jobs well we will create many satisfied customers. They will return to us for future purchases and send their friends to us for purchases who will tell their friends and so on. So you see, it is not about the money, it is about what we do."

She then further demonstrated her point by showing the charitable contributions of the organization to their community. She showed the increase in jobs and the impact the company had overall on the growth of their community by providing employment. She showed how their employees were increasing purchases on everything around them, from business at the barbershop to the amount of food purchased at a local grocery store.

At this point the executives in the room each gave a brief presentation about why they believed so much in the products they made and the services they provided.

"When people call us for service, I want them to know they have called people who care, people who think and work on their behalf all day, every day," offered the CEO.

A Vice President talked about what we want from the goods and services people give us. "We want the best, things that work, services that are easy, and cost effective and do the job they are supposed to do."

"Think of what you would want if you were purchasing from us and then make it happen," added another.

"We are about enhancing the world with our products and services and adding to the quality of life for our customers," chimed in another Vice President.

The meeting concluded with each employee receiving a personalized compensation packet. It explained their current position and pay range, their annual increase potential for the current year and their potential quarterly bonus amount. Sam was surprised to find an additional document in his packet that showed several different promotional career paths that he might want to consider. The document detailed the competencies he needed to be eligible for these promotions and offered suggestions on how to obtain them through classes, in-house training and mentoring. A form to sign up for the company mentoring program was enclosed.

A calendar was included in the packet showing monthly review meetings with his boss, Patrick, and their dates, times and locations. He was also given a performance expectation sheet detailing what was expected of him in the next thirty days.

The meeting adjourned with each executive shaking the hands of the new employees and offering to support them in whatever way they could. Sam noted that each executive had a list in their hands with the employee's name and position. They used this to talk and ask about the specific work that needed to be done by this individual. This gave Sam a sense that they knew how he fit in the organization and what he had to do to be successful. It was both humbling and overwhelming how clear they all were on the work to be done.

Sam was not surprised, as he left for the day, to see the reader board above the exit reiterate, *It's not about the money*.

8

Contribute Something

Sam whistled as he entered his office and began to work on the assignments that he and Patrick discussed. As promised, there was a great deal of information downloaded to his computer and he had a good handle on what and where he should be putting his efforts according to Patrick's instructions.

After a few hours of work, Sam realized this was the second day he had not been greeted at the door to the company as he started his day. He kind of missed it. He even thought back to the bear hug he got on the first day and realized there were worse ways to be welcomed, like being ignored. He made a mental note to greet his fellow employees when he came to work each day.

Sam collaborated with a few colleagues on getting additional information he needed, then headed to the cafeteria to grab a mid-morning snack. Those free energy bars were sounding mighty good to his grumbling stomach.

Several people in the room walked up to him and introduced themselves, noting that his name badge still said "new employee." Sam now knew why there was a gold star on his badge. Everyone wanted to be sure all was well with him. He was offered business cards with notes on the back on how they could help him in the future.

Sam headed back to his office feeling that everyone in the place was there for him. What a great way to work.

He was stopped short when he arrived in his office by his screensaver. It read *Contribute Something*, with an icon marked "click here to find out how." Sam clicked on the icon and was stunned to see the CEO's picture come up on the screen with an accompanying audio.

"Hi," began the CEO, "I am here to talk to you about making a contribution in this organization and in your life. Many people spend a great deal of time trying to find the meaning of life. I don't readily have the answer. I can guess that the meaning is, if we are here on the planet, there is still something for us to do. I believe that when people contribute something to this world in any way, big or small, the world gets better."

"Each day, it is very important that each employee finds a way to contribute something. You probably already saw an example of that today when people you didn't know introduced themselves and offered to help you in the future. Their contribution was to let you know you were not alone and that help was available."

Sam blinked at that statement. How could she possibly have known what just transpired in the cafeteria? The thought of hidden cameras suddenly came to mind, and Sam laughed to himself. The voice continued.

"We often wait for the completion of something big to focus on contribution. But that is not the way we always operate around here. We look for big and small ways to contribute every day. We even check ourselves and keep records of how we are doing. If you will look in the top drawer of your desk you will find a checklist. It has a place for the date and a description of your contribution each day. These are not earth shattering events. Some days our contribution is that we showed up and helped to carry the load. Other days we listen attentively to someone who needs an ear. Then there are days when we really help someone, finish something or solve a problem. There are all manner of ways to contribute. So far, as a new employee, you have contributed by being here, listening to the principles of our work code and agreeing to operate by them. Quite a contribution in your two weeks!"

Now Sam was really spooked. Where was this coming from, and more importantly, where was it going? Was all this just for him or did everyone get this message?

The audio finished with some examples of contributions from other lists. They were large and small, serious and comedic at times (found Jim's socks left in the gym). All in all, it was a very impressive list of examples.

The CEO ended her presentation with another sincere welcome and an apology for the recorded message. She explained that despite the desire for high personal contact, her executive role simply did not allow as much time for these things as she would like. She asked that, when Sam did have the opportunity to meet and speak with her, he use the time to make suggestions and comments she should consider to make the company better.

Sam sat back as the picture left the screen and his original screensaver returned. Gremlins, thought Sam. He opened his top drawer to discover the sheet and saw his start date on the first line. Sam thought, at this rate, he was already behind. He better get cracking.

Throughout the day as Sam found himself in meetings or alone, he looked at how he was contributing. At one meeting he spoke up, even though he feared he was too naïve on the subject, because he felt he had to make a contribution. At the gym he contemplated how being in good shape helped him think clearly because he felt well. When he was alone he kept in mind that his work was one piece in the larger success of his department and the company. By the end of the day he had no trouble knowing he contributed something and recording it on his sheet.

With a smile on his face he passed under the reader board as it read, *Contribute Something.*

9

Work is About Joy

Sam walked into the plant entrance and was immediately struck by the smiles and laughter coming from the production line. The plant manager, Gerald, walked up to Sam as he entered and asked if he could spend a few minutes with him before he headed back to his office. Sam readily agreed and Gerald handed him the required safety gear for his tour. He began by showing him the production line and explaining the various components of the process. Next they went to an area that was used for planning and process improvement. The tour was punctuated with introductions to various people on the line and many smiles.

Sam and Gerald then went into Gerald's office, which had an overview of the floor and cartoon characters stuck to the window.

Gerald then asked Sam a question, "Do you enjoy working?"

Sam was somewhat taken aback, but readily replied that he did, most of the time.

"What is it about your work that you enjoy?" inquired Gerald.

"Well, I like the challenge of the projects I work on, the people I interact with and the money to buy and do things," was Sam's response.

"Good answers," said Gerald. "Now tell me more about what makes work enjoyable for you." Sam was befuddled thinking he had already answered that question, but Gerald was persistent in his question and wanted to know more.

Sam eventually figured he needed a longer list, so he talked about having a good boss that taught him many things. He mentioned that he had the opportunity to learn and to grow both professionally and personally from training programs and that he even learned things from day-to-day interactions with others. He talked about being part of a larger organization, providing goods and services to people that enriched their lives and possibly making the world a better place.

"Very good," exclaimed Gerald, "You really have your hands around the concept of work. For far too long people have come to look at work as a place to get money to do other things, rather than appreciating the work for what it has to offer in our own personal growth and development. At our company all our managers are trained to understand that they have the highest burden on them, that of making work a joy for their staff. People who are taught to appreciate their work, no matter how small or simple the task are people who enjoy life, make the company stronger and provide the best goods and services.

Sadly, many managers have been trained in other companies to administer the rules, increase productivity at the expense of quality and just get things done. While rules have their place, productivity is very important and getting things done a must, there are ways to accomplish all these tasks and keep the worker and the work in a joyful place.

You saw the smiles and heard the laughter on our plant floor today as you came in. The reason that occurred is because we were passing around jokes as a way to start the day. We get a good, clean, funny joke off the internet every day and collect them for 'joke day' once a week. You saw silly sock day last week, and we do many other things to keep the levity high. We also do many things to emphasize safety in the same way. Productivity and the importance of adhering to rules also receive a great deal of attention. These things occur in such a way so that everyone understands why we ask what we do, even if it takes longer to teach or explain. We do all these things in a way that respects and honors the worker. We know they bring knowledge and expertise to us, we know they need to learn more, and we know that they deserve to participate in the success of the company. You saw in the bonus program that these people participate, just as you do in the program and rightfully so. Their work is important."

Sam was impressed with the passion he heard in Gerald's words. He asked if this philosophy was unique or if it was shared by others in the plant.

"It is not my philosophy, it is our philosophy," said Gerald. "All the people who come to work here are asked to demonstrate how they enjoy their work, how they help others enjoy their work and how they will continue to grow while they work here. It is a fundamental principle in working in our company that individual growth and enjoyment of our work must be there for us to serve our customers and be successful."

Sam could not help but ask why. Gerald responded that it was simple. "Our customers and our product are not valued without joy in our work. That means we can make money and still provide a service and a product, but cannot honor either if we are not honoring ourselves first by being joyful in what we do."

Sam sat back and said simply, "I don't get it. I get services from people all the time that don't like their jobs. You can tell by their surly attitudes, how they ignore me and the slow service."

"True," said Gerald, "there are indeed people like that, however my question to you is why do you purchase from them?" As a consumer you should be discerning in your purchasing habits and protect yourself from people who do not want to give you goods or services from their heart. You will only continue to have a bad experience if you continue to do business with them. We own what we do," he continued. "It is our mark in life and we want to do it well and enjoy doing it. This is a very complicated and yet simple concept. It has been lost in America and other parts of the world for so long that we barely understand it anymore. Work has taken on the connotation of labor, servitude, drudgery and many other bad names. In reality it can all be fun. Look around you.

Does any job really have to be bad if we don't want it to be? Garbage collection can be smelly and messy, but you do get to be outdoors, move around a lot and help keep the world cleaner. It pays fairly well for these inconveniences. And with a smile on your face even garbage collection can be enjoyed. Why do we immediately think that only the glitzy jobs can be enjoyed? Why do we think because we are overburdened in our work, under-staffed and under-appreciated that work cannot be enjoyed?"

Gerald went on, "Employees often make the mistake of thinking that if they are not shown appreciation for what they do then they are working in a terrible place. Employers really should be very aware of the contributions of their employees and hand out praise frequently. Employers also need to provide adequate staffing and tools to help get things done effectively. If they do not do all of these, however, I would like to suggest that the employee can still enjoy what they do. They know they do their job well and understand that they are making a contribution in some way to the world. Outside approval is a nice add-on, however, not a necessity. Understaffed situations occur all the time and can present challenges, as well as opportunities. If we don't have every tool in the box, as on the famous Apollo flight to the moon, we improvise and still get things done. The heart of the matter is that the employee knows their work is good, enjoys it and appreciates the opportunity to do it. We need to realize the fact that work is to be enjoyed and then go about finding how it is enjoyable. If someone tells you their job is a terrible place to work, suggest they change employers, the conditions or their attitude toward the conditions and begin enjoying work again."

Gerald was really on a roll now, Sam noticed. Sure enough Gerald jumped in again. "Life is too short not to enjoy the work we do. Some people may have better work situations than others. But you can make almost any situation better with your attitude to make the best of what you have to do. Watch for this enjoying work syndrome to show up in the strangest places. If someone tells you their job is a chore and a

bore, ask what they are doing to change the situation. If they say there is
nothing they can do, challenge them to find ways to change the situation.
Make it a habit to ask people if they enjoy their jobs and when they
answer yes, celebrate with them. When they answer no, implement the
how can you enjoy your work challenge. Quite often I find that some
people don't want to find a way to enjoy their work on purpose. They
love their misery and the stories it provides."

"Now back to you. We want you to enjoy your job. We feel it is our
responsibility to help you enjoy your job. The bottom line is, and always
will be, that only you can make this job enjoyable for yourself. We will
sometimes not have enough staff. Other times systems or tools will be
missing. When we get too busy we may forget to tell you how much we
appreciate what you do. None of these things should keep you from
enjoying your work. You and only you can make that happen. Find out
how to work around short staffing. Find creative ways to work without
all the systems or tools. Know in your heart that you have done well
and congratulate yourself when we forget. Smile when you think of your
work. Enjoy your work. It is your life."

Sam left Gerald and headed back to his office. Along the way he
noticed people who really seemed to be enjoying what they were doing.
He noticed a couple that seemed a bit frustrated at the moment, and he
wondered if they were enjoying their jobs. He then remembered that not
everything would go perfectly all the time, and the name of the game was
to enjoy your job overall. Not every minute can be perfect. The fun part
about this concept was that overall it could be very enjoyable, with those
pit stops of frustration just being short points in time along the way.

Sam finished his day by going around the company and thanking
everyone who had helped him through this most unusual orientation. His
last stop was at Dottie's desk. He smiled as he approached her and held
out his hand.

"Thank you for that wonderful bear hug you gave me last week. It taught me a very valuable lesson that I won't forget. You see, I am not the hugging kind of guy and actually did not think that it was the right thing to do for a new employee. Now I know that you were being honest with me about how you felt about me joining the company. I know you enjoy your job and want others to enjoy it too, and when we are that happy and that joyful we usually give someone a big hug. We do it at weddings and birthdays and other celebrations. You showed me that working is a celebration. Not just here, but anywhere that I choose to contribute. Thank you for that most valuable lesson."

Dottie smiled and looked at Sam and said, "You know when I started here, I would never have guessed that work could be such a joy. I am not doing work that is substantially different than the last company I worked for here at the Top Banana Institute. The big difference here is that I know how to see my work with joy. I know those around me are giving their best, contributing, trusting, welcoming new ideas, taking care of themselves and me. I appreciate the kind words that my boss gives me all the time about my work and I know that even when he forgets that I am capable of giving them to myself. I'm glad you are here, and I am glad that I am here."

As Sam left that day the read out board simply said, *We hope you will enjoy your work.*

10

Appreciation and Positive Thinking

Sam headed into the office on the last day of his second week full of ideas and thoughts. He had a major project that he would be responsible for in the coming weeks, and several people had been assigned with him on the project. His position was team leader, and he wanted to be a good leader. He decided that before he started his day he would stop by and ask his boss Patrick for a few words of wisdom on leading others. He had heard about the Top Banana Management CD's everyone was listening to and thought this might be a good time to start doing that himself.

Patrick smiled as he saw Sam in the doorway and beckoned him into his office and to a chair. "How can I help you today" he inquired of Sam. Sam explained that he was looking for some advice on being a good leader for the project team he was heading.

Patrick paused for a few minutes and then smiled at Sam and said, "Thank you."

Sam waited and when nothing else came he looked at Patrick and said, "What do you mean thank you?"

Patrick then explained to Sam that a good leader knows one thing; employees, colleagues, customers and vendors only wish for one thing: some appreciation. Appreciation that is accomplished in the simplest of ways, through small rewards, recognition of what has been done and a simple thank you.

Patrick elaborated for Sam, "We have so much going on all

around us each day, and we are so busy that we forget that we need the nourishment of appreciation. We don't always want it from just our supervisor or boss. We need it from colleagues, customers and even vendors. One of the things we practice here is always finding a way every day to let someone in this organization, a customer, client or vendor know that we appreciate them. This is the heart of what we do. This is the reason we are successful, even with all the other great things we have shown you so far."

"Our people understand that a quick email, a voice mail message, a note, a passing word in the hall, all add up to let people know that we appreciate the things they do all day, every day in a thousand different ways."

"Think of it this way, each morning an employee or even a customer is like an empty water glass. All day long we fill our water glasses to give our body the nourishment it needs to support our life. Appreciation supports and nourishes our work. I want to see something in your glass and the glasses of all those around you that you can use to nourish you when things go wrong. I want to nourish your spirit when your energy is down and to nourish you when you don't know where to turn next because you have so much to do. Not having this sense of appreciation throughout the day is like being thirsty all day. You can still function, however it isn't as easy."

Sam paused for a moment and then asked, "Isn't the roll of appreciation really something managers do? Don't we tell the manager's about their employees and then let them pass along the good news? Particularly so the manager will give credit to this person."

Patrick smiled and laughed, "You know Sam, you just hit on the fundamental problem running around in our culture and our companies. We think someone else should do it. Whether it is praise or a correction, we think someone else should do it. It is our job, it is our responsibility. In a restaurant, at work, at the grocery store, at the club, we need to be conscious of the importance of appreciation and what it means to those who are working beside us and on our behalf."

Sam thought about this a minute and got a little uneasy. He felt that he was pretty good at saying thank you on a regular basis and wondered what was missing. As if reading his thoughts Patrick piped up, "We are all good at saying thank you for service or a helping hand. However, what we are talking about here is going beyond the simple thank you now and then, to consciously reinforcing with people all the time that we appreciate them.

Patrick continued on, "Let me ask you, you have been here two weeks, how many phone calls, emails and gold stars have you received?"

Sam didn't take long to reply, "About a hundred it seems. Every time I pick up voice mail there is someone saying thanks about the simplest of things. My email each morning and all day will have a short quip of thanks from someone and I have a mountain of those gold stars in a pile on my desk."

"Have you received any Top Bananas yet," asked Patrick.

"I did," replied Sam excitedly, "those are really cool!"

"You see how excited you are over a silly little squeezable banana," said Patrick. "This is what appreciation does to people. It takes away stress, it creates excitement and it energizes people to want to come back, do more, try again and so on."

Sam said, "I think I am starting to get it. You really believe that all this positive reinforcement and feedback will really make a difference in how we view our work and our day."

"Absolutely," said Patrick, "We know you need the nourishment of being appreciated, and we work hard to fill that glass that holds your appreciation so you will enjoy your job."

"What is really important to remember here, is that anyone can do this for anyone else, we don't have rules here about who hands out gold stars. Those stars you are receiving are coming from the janitor, the president, your colleagues, anyone and everyone. Some people have their calendars programmed to take a break and say thank you. I've heard people say this gives them more of a boost than the person receiving the star. I think that is true, because I feel that way every time I stop to appreciate someone. It seems to do as much or more for me than for them." Patrick was truly animated as he spoke about this thought. Patrick continued, "This is really the power behind our appreciation program here, it has no rules, there are no monetary rewards, you don't get ten stars and trade them for a prize, the prize is in the thought itself and the fact that someone took the time to appreciate your efforts. We think this has value beyond measure."

Patrick then asked Sam if he had observed people walking around the company with banana books.

"I have," said Sam, "I wasn't really sure what they were and to be honest was a little afraid to ask. They seemed to be something personal, like a diary."

"Pretty close," said Patrick. "We keep books around us that have lists of the positive things about people. If you happened to open one of them you would find a first name at the top of the page and then lists of positive things about this person. Mine starts with my kids and my wife and then has my bosses, my employees, my colleagues, my mailperson and much more. At any point in time, one of these people can do something that will probably upset me or make me unhappy. People just do that. To put it in perspective, I glance at their page, and my view of the situation usually changes pretty dramatically on the spot."

"Does that really work," Sam asked.

"You would be amazed," replied Patrick. "Let me tell you a true story in our company about this program. One of our managers had an employee that was really a poor fit for his job. Over time the work in his area had changed and when he needed to move to the next level with the work, he just was unable to master it, despite an incredible effort on his part and everyone around him. His manager was terribly dismayed, as dismissal was inevitable. Rather than agonizing over the decision the manager took four days and worked really hard next to this person, noting in his banana book after each of these encounters the positive and good things about this person. Some days it wasn't even work related. He would write that he showed up on time, dressed neatly, answered phone calls quickly, smiled often and was cordial to everyone he encountered. On the fifth day the employee walked into his office and offered his resignation. When manager asked why, the employee responded that he was not good at what the manager was now asking him to do and The Manager deserved someone better on his team. The employee also said that he knew he could be successful in a different job more suited to what he did best. Note that last comment. The manager's attention and focus on the positive aspects of this person allowed him to keep his self esteem in tact, recognize he did have skills and abilities and that they could be utilized somewhere. Pretty powerful, don't you agree?"

Sam sat in his chair stunned. He was sure he had never seen an approach of this nature to a failing employee.

"What if he hadn't quit," asked Sam. "That could very possibly happen. People can cling to a miserable situation for a long time immobilized by the fear of finding another job or that they are even capable of another job. Sadly, should that happen," Patrick replied, "the employee would go through our performance enhancement program where we would explain that we have areas they must master, with our help of course, in a specific period of time, or they will be asked to leave the company. During that time we also focus on their strengths in great detail, pointing to the types of work that are more suited to their situation. We do then follow through with termination if they are unable to perform in the tasks assigned. You would be surprised how often we don't need to do this. The self awareness created in showing people what they do well, as compared to what they do not do well, is very energizing in getting people to look for where they can work that they will be successful and happy."

Sam and Patrick chatted for a few more minutes while Patrick offered some ideas on how to recognize the new project team on a regular basis. As Sam stood to leave, Patrick handed him a banana book. "I think you are ready for this now," said Patrick. Sam smiled and thought to himself that he had a lot of entries to make about the incredible people he had met in the last two weeks. He also thought he might throw in the name of the guy who was fixing the leak in his apartment. Over the past few days the work hadn't gone perfectly. However, he had seen many good qualities in this repair person and knew he could probably put some water in his glass with a few kind words.

Sam left that day curious to see what the reader board would have for him on this subject. Why was he not surprised to see, *Thank You.*

11

It is a Better Workplace

It was a sunny morning as Sam pulled into the parking lot to begin his work day. His orientation had ended Friday, and he felt well on his way with both work and his integration into the new company. Sam pondered over an interesting and wonderful two weeks as he pulled into his employee of the year parking space. He thought about the many things he had been exposed to and had learned and knew he had found the right job. He congratulated himself on taking the chance and making the change to a work environment where he knew he would be happy. He chuckled to himself over that bear hug he received on the first day. He now understood the enthusiasm he felt from everyone over the past two weeks.

Sam thought about how the different concepts he had learned came together to help him approach both the people and the situations he would encounter. He reflected on how good it felt to remove diminishing comments from his language. Sam knew he was responsible for good outcomes in his work. Sam knew people would not be judging how he worked as long as he achieved the outcomes that were expected. He noticed that he was now checking himself before he made a judgment of others' choices. All these changes were creating a greater sense of ease in his work. Best of all, his mind seemed less concerned with fixing others' perceptions and thoughts! He loved being trusted by everyone and found himself working diligently not to let others down. Sam was ready to trust and be trusted. It felt so simple and comfortable compared to waiting for trust to be earned or watching others to see if he could trust them.

Sam now knew how to add to the ideas of others and with this he seemed to be getting smarter and smarter in his work. It was easy to see his contribution to the organization, thanks to the charting he was doing. It amazed Sam how much more content he was at the end of the day with the knowledge that, even in little things, he was contributing.

Sam was pleased to feel that he would work in an environment that listened to his ideas, no matter how unconventional or maybe even impossible they sounded. Knowing he could speak freely felt good and he knew he would honor that gift by being thoughtful in what he offered. Sam laughed as he thought about a few of the mistakes he had made in the past week and the exercise of learning what gifts they had brought him. He was surprised at how much he learned and improved in that process.

Sam had had some fun at the gym, took a yoga class and found himself in the playroom once when he just couldn't focus on a really tough issue. Sam knew that how he viewed his physical, mental, and spiritual health made a big difference in what he had to give to both the company and himself. All of these had helped him keep up his energy and clarify his thinking around issues at work.

Sam knew in his heart it wasn't just about the money. Sure, money was needed. However, he also knew he really wanted the products and services he helped deliver to be the best. Sam knew deep down he wanted people to be pleased with the results of his work, and he knew he wanted them to be steady customers. When Sam received his first paycheck, he smiled at the thought that people saw, appreciated, bought and used their products and services. He knew they would continue to do so, as the employees gave their all in making these products and services the best.

After two weeks at his new job Sam felt transformed and elated. He began to think of the challenge placed before him to not only work with a new attitude, but to live with a new attitude. He marveled at the opportunity to see and be at work with harmony, peace and play as criteria for getting things done. Sam realized that honoring play and playfulness in his work and life would bring the gift of joy to all he did.

As Sam walked into the office, he realized that coming to work was now like a breath of fresh air. Sam knew most of all that he was appreciated for what he did. Sam also knew he had a responsibility to appreciate others and would never again take that responsibility lightly.

Sam's final thought as he entered the door was how easy it was to have a peaceful, respectful and productive work environment. He now knew that work could be a joy.

About the Author

Barbara Brannen is a Human Resources Executive and nationally acclaimed speaker with over 30 years of experience and playfulness under her belt. She has served as Vice-President and a member of the executive team for such organizations as Qwest Communications, Rose Medical Center, AON/Innovative Services of America and the University of Denver. Barbara has been recognized as the Human Resource Professional of the Year in 1990 by the Colorado Human Resources Association and was named as an Outstanding Woman in Business in Human Resources for 2002 by the Denver Business Journal.

Barbara is a keynote speaker and consults with businesses as a Human Resource Strategist. Barbara is answering the question of how we can be more successful in our businesses and in our lives. She is the author of the book, *Office Peace – Your Guide to a More Respectful (and More Productive) Work Environment* and the book, *The Gift of Play*. Barbara is a member of the National Speakers Association. Her unique programs have been instituted at organizations from large technology firms to hospitals and construction companies.

Her work is designed to increase cooperation, creativity and energy in individuals and teams, while putting more black ink on the bottom line.

Barbara's clients enjoy her energy and creativity and always end up having more fun than before she came.

Ask Barbara
to speak
at your next event!
Call 303-984-9271

Playmore™ Products Order Form

CAUTION! Only purchase the following if you are willing to have fun and enjoy your time at work and play!

❑ **Book** *Office Peace – Your Guide to a More Respectful (and More Productive!) Work Environment*
　　1-25　　　$15.00 each
　　25-100　　$12.00 each
　　100-500　$10.00 each
　　　　　　　_____ Qty.　_____ Total Cost

❑ **Book** *The Gift of Play*
　$15.00 Each
　　　　　　　_____ Qty.　_____ Total Cost

❑ **CD Set** Top Banana Management Series
(12 CDs **$299.00**)
　　　　　　　_____ Qty.　_____ Total Cost

❑ **DVD** *Learning to Play More to Keep from Turning to Crispy Burnt Toast*
$12.00 each
　　　　　　　_____ Qty.　_____ Total Cost

❑ **Mem-Cards™** *Office Peace*
$10.00 each
　　　　　　　_____ Qty.　_____ Total Cost

_____ Subtotal

_____ Sales Tax 4.6%
(Colorado residents)

_____ Shipping

_____ **TOTAL**

Payment: ❑ Check ❑ MasterCard ❑ Visa

Account Number: _____ Expiration Date: _____

Name on Card: _____

Playmore™ Products Order Form

Please fill out the following:

Your name or any other information will never be sold to anyone else, ever.
It will only be used for order processing and to inform you of future books and merchandise.

Name: _____

Address: _____

_____

City: _____ State/Province: _____

Postal Code: _____

Telephone: _____

E-mail: _____

Online Orders: www.letsplaymore.com
Fax Orders: 303-973-3041
Telephone Orders: 303-984-9271
                        (Please have your credit card ready.)
Postal Orders: Playmore
                        11988 West Cooper Drive
                        Littleton, Colorado 80127

100% Satisfaction Guaranteed. No questions asked. Full Refund.

Ask Barbara to speak at your next event!
Call 303-984-9271

Visit our website for FREE information on :
More fun and playful things to do, speaking/seminars, mailing lists, and personal and professional coaching. Find out how you can contribute to the Quest for World Peace.